SUPER
SANDCASTLE
Super Simple Crafts

SUPER SIMPLE
Magnets

Fun and Easy-to-Make
Crafts for Kids

Karen Latchana Kenney

Consulting Editor, Diane Craig, M.A./Reading Specialist

ABDO
Publishing Company

Published by ABDO Publishing Company, 8000 West 78th Street, Edina, Minnesota 55439.
Copyright © 2010 by Abdo Consulting Group, Inc. International copyrights reserved in all
countries. No part of this book may be reproduced in any form without written permission from
the publisher. Super SandCastle™ is a trademark and logo of ABDO Publishing Company.

Printed in the United States.

Editor: Liz Salzmann
Content Developer: Nancy Tuminelly
Cover and Interior Design and Production: Oona Gaarder-Juntti, Mighty Media
Photo Credits: Colleen Dolphin, Shuttterstock
Activity Production: Oona Gaarder-Juntti, Pam Scheunemann

The following manufacturers/names appearing in this book are trademarks:
Plaid® Mod Podge®, Office Depot® Posterboard, Elmer's® Glue-All™,
Crayola® Washable Glitter Glue, Scotch® Masking Tape, Sanford® Sharpie®

Library of Congress Cataloging-in-Publication Data

Kenney, Karen Latchana.
  Super simple magnets : fun and easy-to-make crafts for kids / Karen Latchana Kenney.
    p. cm. -- (Super simple crafts)
  ISBN 978-1-60453-626-3
  1. Handicraft--Juvenile literature. 2. Magnets--Juvenile literature. I. Title.

TT160.K424 2010
745.59--dc22
                      2009000355

Super SandCastle™ books are created by a team of professional educators, reading
specialists, and content developers around five essential components—phonemic awareness,
phonics, vocabulary, text comprehension, and fluency—to assist young readers as they develop
reading skills and strategies and increase their general knowledge. All books are written,
reviewed, and leveled for guided reading, early reading intervention, and Accelerated Reader®
programs for use in shared, guided, and independent reading and writing activities
to support a balanced approach to literacy instruction.

To Adult Helpers

Making magnets is fun and simple to do. There are just a few things
to remember to keep kids safe. Sometimes baking in an oven is
required. For those activities, adult supervision is needed. Also,
glue, paint, and markers will be used in some activities. Make sure
kids protect their clothes and work surfaces before starting.

Table of Contents

Symbols

Look for these symbols in this book.

Super Hot. Be careful! You will be
working with something that is super
hot. Ask an adult to help you.

Adult Help. Get help! You will need
help from an adult.

Magnetic Art!

What's so cool about making magnets? It's art that sticks to things! Foam, **felt**, and even bottle caps can become magnets. It's simple. Make flowers, bugs, and picture frames. Then stick them on your refrigerator. Try some or all of the **projects** in this book. It's up to you. From start to finish, making super simple magnets is fun to do!

Tools and Supplies

Here are many of the things you will need to do the **projects** in this book. You can find them online or at your local craft store.

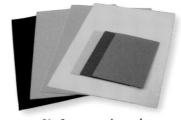

craft foam sheets

colorful paper

paintbrushes

feathers

acrylic paint

sequins

felt

flat clear glass marbles

rhinestones

metal bottle caps

ribbon

jar

3D paint

wax paper

stickers

Styrofoam balls

magnets

googly eyes

wooden craft spoons

Mod Podge

wooden spring clothespins

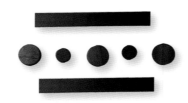
rubber stamps

poster board

foam stickers

glue

glitter glue

polymer clay

masking tape

pipe cleaners

small unpainted
wooden frame

Mystery Marbles

Look into these marbles to see the pictures inside!

Supply List
- magnet
- flat clear glass marble
- pencil
- poster board
- scissors
- magazines
- glue

1. Use a magnet that is a little bit smaller than the marble. Trace the magnet onto poster board. Cut it out.

2. Look through the magazines. Find a cool picture. Put the marble over it to see how it looks. Place the poster board shape over the picture you chose. Trace around the poster board and cut out the picture.

3. Glue the picture on top of the poster board shape. Let the glue dry.

4. Glue the front of the picture to the flat side of the marble. Don't worry! The glue will be clear when it is dry.

5. Glue the magnet to the poster board. Let the glue dry.

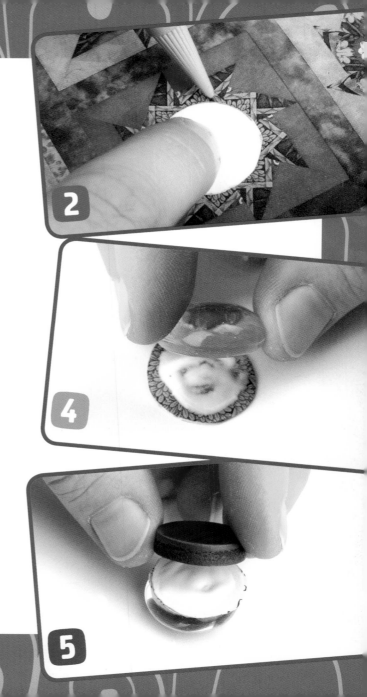

Recycled Bottle Caps

These magnets make cool gifts and help the earth!

1 Wash the bottle caps with soap and water. Be sure they are dry before continuing.

2 Cut out a square of poster board a little larger than the quarter. Put the quarter on the square and trace around it.

3 Make a straight cut across the poster board to the circle. Cut out the circle.

4 Tape the edges of the straight cut back together. This circle is the same size as the inside of a bottle cap.

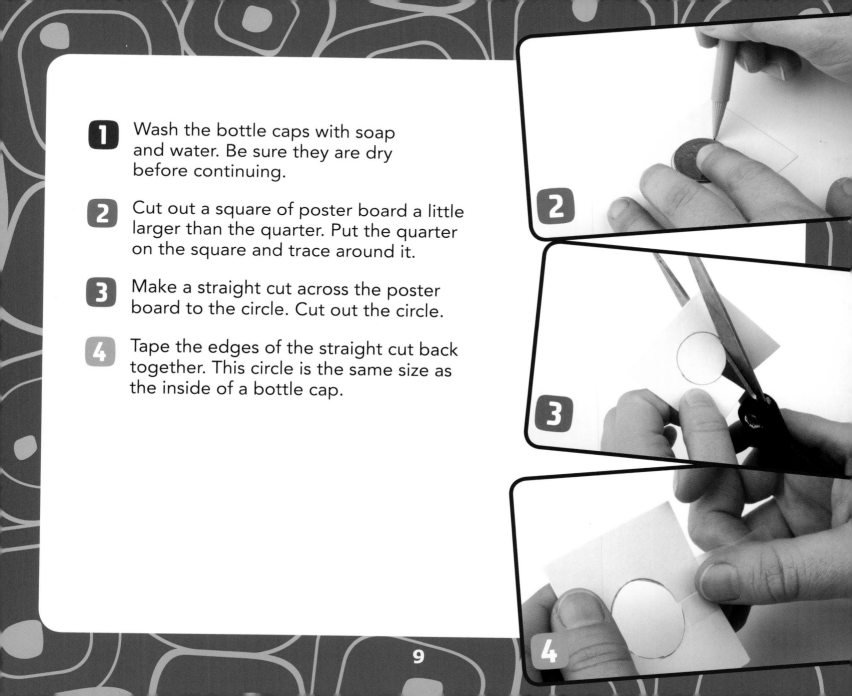

5 Look for a small picture for your magnet. Use the circle you cut out as a frame. Put it over the picture to see how it will look.

6 Trace around the picture you want to use. Cut it out.

7 Glue the picture inside a bottle cap. Smooth it out to get rid of bubbles. Let the glue dry.

8 Cover the picture with Mod Podge. This will **protect** the picture. Let the Mod Podge dry.

9 Put a thin line of glitter glue around the edge of the picture. Let it dry.

10 Glue a magnet to the back of the bottle cap. Let the glue dry.

Twisty Bugs

Play around with the twisty legs on these silly bugs!

Supply List

- small Styrofoam ball
- knife
- acrylic paint
- paintbrush
- pen
- poster board
- scissors
- glue
- pipe cleaner
- googly eyes
- strip magnet

1. Ask an adult to cut the Styrofoam ball in half.

2. Use one half for the body of the bug. Paint it a bright color or make a pattern. Let the paint dry.

3. Trace the shape of the body onto a piece of poster board. Cut it out. Glue the poster board to the flat side of the body.

4. Cut a pipe cleaner into eight pieces. Six will be the legs and two will be the antennae.

5. Stick the legs into the sides of the body. Curl the ends of the two antennae. Stick them in the front of the body.

6. Glue the googly eyes above the antennae.

7. Stick a strip magnet to the back of the bug.

Crazy Clothespins

Make magnet pins to hold your messages!

14

1. Paint the top, sides, and inside of the clothespin. Don't paint the back. Don't worry about getting paint on the spring. Any paint on the spring can be rubbed off when it's dry.

2. When the paint is dry, decorate the clothespin. Use your imagination to decide how to decorate it. You can use things like foam stickers, glitter glue, or more paint. Try gluing some ribbon along the top. Be creative!

3. Wait for any glue or paint used in decorating to dry completely. Glue a magnet to the back of the clothespin.

Flutter Fairies

It's fun to make pretty little fairies with your friends!

Supply List

- scrap paper
- scissors
- craft foam
- wooden craft spoon
- glue
- markers
- feathers
- rhinestones
- ribbon
- glitter glue
- strip magnet

16

1. Draw the shape of the fairy's wings onto scrap paper. Cut them out. Trace the paper wings onto foam. Cut out the foam wings.

2. Glue the foam wings to the middle of the craft spoon.

3. Turn the fairy so the spoon faces up. Use markers to draw the eyes, nose, and mouth.

4. Glue some feathers above the eyes. Cut a small strip of foam. Stick a rhinestone in the middle of the strip. This is the fairy's crown. Glue it to the fairy's head.

5. Glue pieces of ribbon to the stick below the mouth. The ribbons should cover the stick to make the fairy's dress.

6. Put glitter glue around the edges of the wings. Let it dry.

7. Stick a magnet to the middle of the fairy's back.

Breezy Butterflies

Make these magnets to hold all your flyers!

Supply List

- 2 wooden craft spoons
- acrylic paint
- paintbrush
- glue
- 3D paint
- glitter glue
- craft foam
- pencil
- scissors
- pipe cleaners
- googly eyes
- round magnet

1. Paint two wooden craft spoons. Be sure to paint the edges of the spoons. Let the paint dry.

2. Glue the spoons together to form the butterfly's wings. Let the glue dry.

3. Decorate the wings with paint, 3D paint, and glitter glue. You can make dots, lines, circles, or any pattern you wish. Let the paint and glue dry.

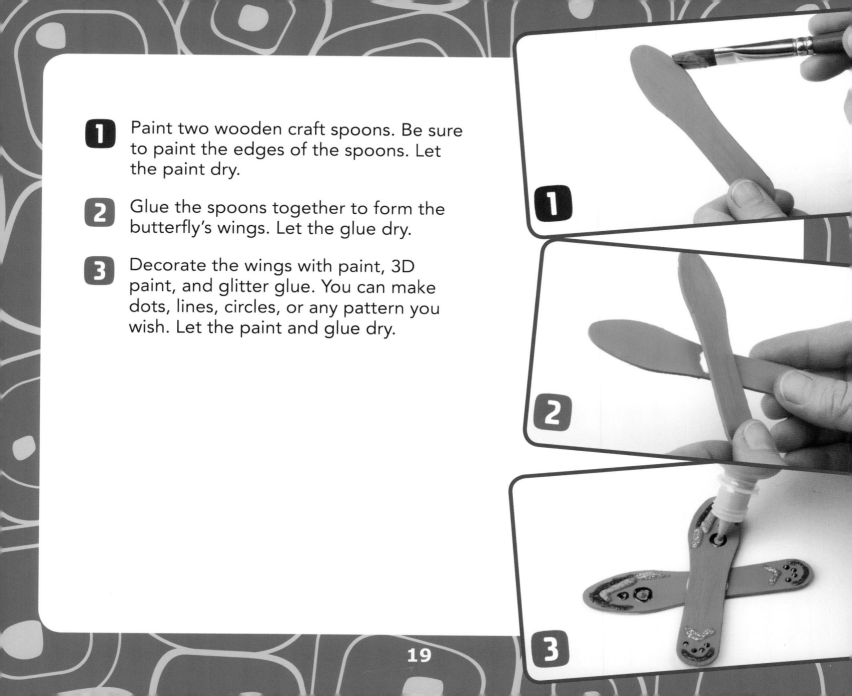

4 Use a pencil to draw the butterfly's body on foam. It should be shaped like the top of an **exclamation point**. Make the body about 2 inches (5 cm) long. If you draw on black foam, the pencil line will show.

5 Cut out the body shape.

6 Cut a piece of pipe cleaner about 4 inches (10 cm) long.

7 Fold the pipe cleaner piece in half. Bend the ends to make them curl. These are the antennae.

8 Glue the antennae to the top of the body. Let the glue dry.

9 Glue the body onto the craft spoons. Let the glue dry.

10 Glue googly eyes onto the body.

11 Glue a round magnet on the back side. Let the glue dry.

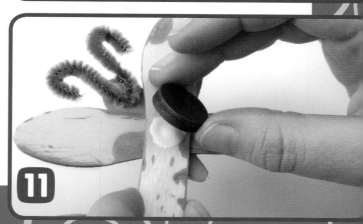

Terrific Tiles

Make tiny tiles for any occasion!

1. Place wax paper over your work area. Use masking tape to secure all four sides.

2. Take about half of a block of the clay. Work it with your hands until it is soft and smooth.

3. Make the clay into a ball. Use the jar to roll the clay out. Stop rolling when it is about ¼ inch (½ cm) thick.

4. Press a rubber stamp firmly into the clay. Remove the stamp.

5. Use a small piece of poster board to cut out the tile. **Repeat** steps 2–5 to make more **terrific** tiles!

6. Put the tiles on a cookie sheet covered with wax paper. Have an adult help you bake the tiles. Follow the directions that came with the clay. Let the tiles cool. Stick a magnet to the back of each tile.

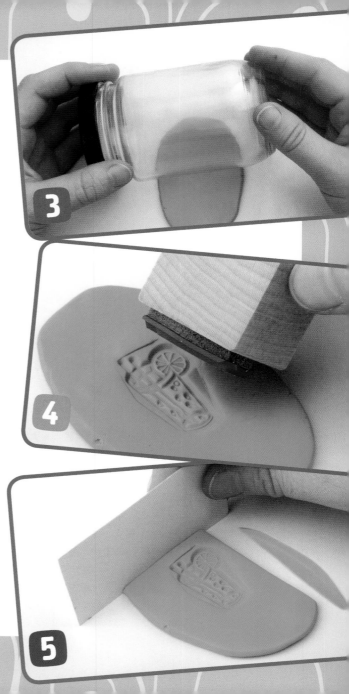

Fun Frames

Your pictures make these magnet frames super special!

1. Choose a picture for your frame. Make sure it fits the frame.

2. Paint the front of the frame. Paint the inside and outside edges too. Let the paint dry.

3. Decorate the frame. Use things such as paint, stickers, foam stickers, and glitter glue. Make a fun **design**.

4. Put your picture on the back side of the frame. Make sure it looks good from the front! Use tape at the top and bottom to hold the picture in place.

5. Stick two strip magnets to the back of the frame. Put the magnets on the two longer sides of the frame.

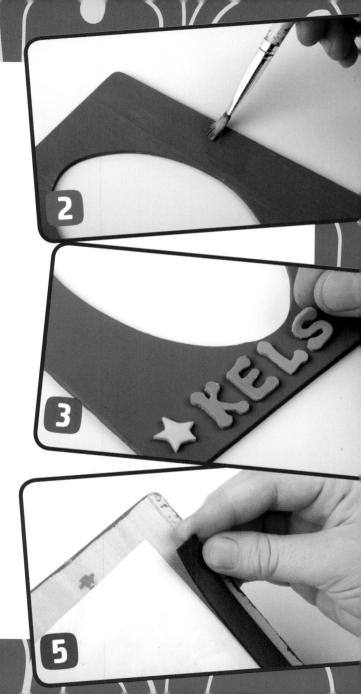

Fuzzy Flowers

These fun magnets are made from fuzzy felt!

Supply List
- felt
- scissors
- poster board
- glue
- strip magnets
- glitter glue (optional)
- sequins (optional)
- 3D paint (optional)

26

1. Cut a piece of **felt** into the shape of a flower. It should be at least 2 inches (5 cm) across.

2. Choose a different color of felt. Cut out a circle smaller than the flower shape. Cut little triangles around the edge.

3. Choose a third color of felt. Cut out a circle that is smaller than the second circle.

4. Cut out a circle of poster board. It should be a little smaller than the first flower shape you made.

5. Glue the felt pieces to the poster board. Go from largest to smallest.

6. Stick two strip magnets to the back.

7. Decorate the flower. Use decorations such as glitter glue, sequins, and 3D paint. Let the glue and paint dry completely.

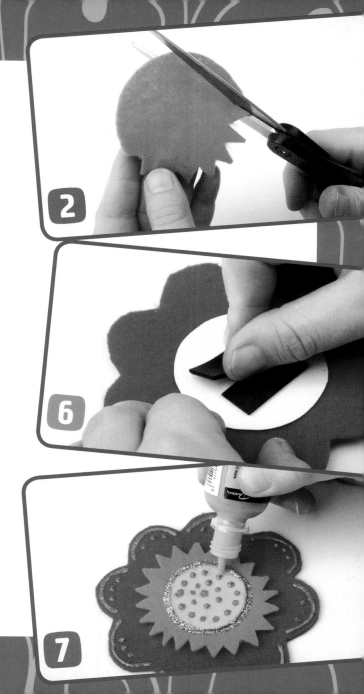

Holiday Time

Celebrate the holidays with cute foam magnets!

Supply List

- scrap paper
- pencil
- scissors
- craft foam
- markers
- strip magnets
- googly eyes
- glue
- glitter glue
- poster board
- feathers
- pipe cleaners
- stapler

CALL ME

BE MINE

COOL CAT

Candy Heart

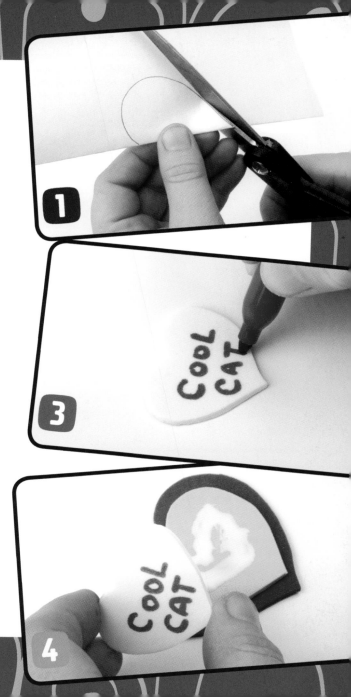

1 Fold a piece of scrap paper in half. Draw half a heart on it at the fold. Cut it out. Make two more hearts. Each heart should be a different size.

2 Open up the hearts. Trace the largest heart onto red foam. Trace the **middle-sized** heart onto pink foam. Trace the smallest heart onto white foam. Cut out the hearts.

3 Write a Valentine's Day message on the white heart. Use a red marker. Make up your own saying.

4 Glue the hearts to each other. The red heart should be on the bottom. The white one should be on the top.

5 Stick a magnet to the back. Now it's time to **celebrate** Valentine's Day!

Spooky Ghost

1 Practice drawing ghosts on scrap paper. Cut out your favorite one. Trace the ghost shape on white foam. Cut out the ghost.

2 Glue on googly eyes. Draw a mouth below the eyes with a black marker.

3 Put glitter glue around the edge of the ghost. Let the glue dry.

4 Stick a magnet strip on the back of the ghost.

Wacky Turkey

1 For the body, cut a large circle out of dark brown foam. For the head, cut a small circle out of light brown foam. Trace the larger circle onto poster board and cut it out.

2 Cut a triangle out of yellow foam for the beak. Cut the turkey's **wattle** out of red foam. Glue all of the foam pieces together. Glue on the googly eyes.

3 Cut the tips off of several feathers. Glue the feathers to the poster board circle.

4 Cut a 3-inch (8-cm) piece of pipe cleaner. Bend it in half. Cut 2 pieces 1½ inches (4 cm) long. Twist the small pieces around the ends of the bent piece. **Staple** the legs to the poster board.

5 Glue the body and face on top of the feathers and legs. Let the glue dry. Stick a magnet to the back.

Glossary

celebrate – to honor with special ceremonies or festivities.

design – a decorative pattern or arrangement.

exclamation point – a punctuation mark that has a vertical line over a dot. It is used after a shouted statement.

felt – a soft, thick fabric.

middle-sized – not the largest or the smallest.

project – a task or activity.

protect – to guard someone or something from harm or danger.

repeat – to do or say something again.

staple – to use a stapler to fasten something together with a thin wire.

terrific – great or wonderful.

wattle – the flap of skin that hangs from the neck of some birds.

About SUPER SANDCASTLE™

Bigger Books for Emerging Readers
Grades K–4

Created for library, classroom, and at-home use, Super SandCastle™ books support and engage young readers as they develop and build literacy skills and will increase their general knowledge about the world around them. Super SandCastle™ books are an extension of SandCastle™, the leading preK–3 imprint for emerging and beginning readers. Super SandCastle™ features a larger trim size for more reading fun.

Let Us Know
Super SandCastle™ would like to hear your stories about reading this book. What was your favorite page? Was there something hard that you needed help with? Share the ups and downs of learning to read. We want to hear from you! Send us an e-mail.

sandcastle@abdopublishing.com

Contact us for a complete list of SandCastle™, Super SandCastle™, and other nonfiction and fiction titles from ABDO Publishing Company.

www.abdopublishing.com • 8000 West 78th Street Edina, MN 55439 • 800-800-1312 • 952-831-1632 fax